Dead Orchids

Kitty Jarman

Dead Orchids

Published by Munger Publishing, Batavia, IL

ISBN: 978-0692825334 (Paperback)

Contents

Acknowledgments

No book is made of pen and paper alone. This collection of poems was reviewed by Writer Groups or other writers and my daughters. They were helpful giving breath to my words. Thanks to the St Charles Library Writers Group, the Batavia Writers Workshop, Fox Valley Writers Group and Writers Anonymous. Thanks to Kevin Moriarity who helped me with the book creation process. Heartfelt thanks to:

Jennie Garmon
Julie Stein
Frank Rutledge
Brandon Fink

Special appreciation goes out to Paul Cook. He wrote very unhelpful critiques on my poems but he loved my writing. And to his wife Susan Cook, the first real life muse I ever met.

Mahalo

Dedication

This book is dedicated

to

Family – Friends

&

Orphans

Artistic Slant

This is my letter to the world
that never wrote to me
the simple news that nature told
with tender majesty.

Her message is committed
to hands I cannot see
for love of her sweet countrymen
judge tenderly of me.

- Emily Dickinson

Dead Orchids

Parchment petals lie on a shelf
bunched like crumpled leaves of fall
dirty whites and faded rose
little girl altar in the hall

I mourn the sad little pieces
like I mourned my mother's life
phalaenopsis was her favorite
the moth, entwined with strife

Years go by and I still try
growing those plants I recall
wondering now not why they died

but why I crave them at all

Loud Painting

She titled it, Barking Canvas.

Three dogs, huge, looking ancient bred,
black blobs tongues a splash of red,
attempting to jump that white picket fence.

Where a little girl stands before a snow
covered evergreen, off center, but still
a lovely winter scene. Her tiny hands
held up to cover her ears, blue eyes
stare wide at you with fear,

while the open mouths
of the artist's dogs
keep barking and barking,
ferociously barking.

A Sonnet, Sad

Gaze on leaves beyond that window sill
Watch them sway to nature's will
Just as he swayed telling me
His love had died unfortunately
I saw his anguish as if he wished
It not to be but it was finished
Distressed I could not stifle a moan
And marvel how he reached to hold
Me least I fall instead I cried
For then I knew - to love is to die
Old age sees the hurt of that day
As a start of a long life of pain

Karmic justice from selfish past lives
Or just fate's wicked throw of the die

Indigenous Dream

lightning bolts stab the top of the Mesa
as a full moon
rises above red rock

he paces in front of me
four feathers braided into one
rope of hair hanging down his
muscled back

walking through a field
of swaying sweet grass

he turns to brush my cheek
with fingers as long
as arrows

I am your Geronimo
he whispers
glancing skyward

before he prances away
as if scout dancing
at a tribal pow wow

scattering my indigenous
dream like smoke signals
fading in an old western

Out of Print

before rough actions of life
destroyed my book's
cover revealing my story's
meaning I lived fully
within the bindings

now I lie naked and exposed

marking time with tired
pages bound by layers
of dust waiting
for someone to pick me up
invest in second hand words

Interstate Driving

three yellowed sheets
of lined paper batter
a frigid wind while
straining against a living
fence of dogwood
bushes growing beside
a busy highway
as if trying
to reach tall
weathered corn
stalks appearing
to stand guard
under a cold
November sun

Carcass In The Snow

After reading a poem about a pony
misplaced during a snowstorm in Colorado
I thought about those cowboys
who plow forward through frigid
canyons on muscled mares cupping
their mouths yelling into the white
night the name of the lost
one as if a precious child.

Back at the ranch before a blazing
fire they will season themselves
to finding the dead carcass
in the spring thaw downing
shots of whisky to numb images
of death while they speak
of mending fences.

The lonely ones will gallop into town
seeking a Miss Kitty for company
so they won't feel the bite
of the wind as it chills the life
of one lost pony.

Diving on Lake Winnebago

We find a body half an hour in
sitting cross legged with two braids
that sway in murky currents
his open eyes revel nothing

The flesh looks real as if mouth to mouth
resuscitation could bring him back

The only sound is the hiss of oxygen
tanks as my diving partner motions
frantically for us to surface

We are not very deep and I keep
moving my feet aware we need
to analyze our next move

Overcome by emotion
I slash tangled fishing line
that bind both ankles
watch the body tilt as it floats
upward towards the surface
where white cranes are feeding

Popcorn

last night's popcorn in a bowl
has the same salty taste
but it was the first
time with you

this morning
your lingering scent
on my skin
teases like silken
corn tassels
swaying in an
evening breeze

loving you feels like
fields of sweet corn
clinging to sunlight
at dusk

Inhale

my sense of self
is resilient
but no one lives
forever

I climb
the highest hill
in the county

speak my name
one
hundred
times

a gentle breeze
disperses the words
to humanity

Concrete Poems

I don't think inside the box,

I don't think outside the box,

I don't even know where the box is!

- Unknown

A Good Heart

The roundness of it surprises
me as I watch the coroner put it into
a vessel. He warns me it is not pretty. Then
describes the injuries inflicted on my husband's body
from the drunk driver in a red pickup truck hitting his
motorcycle as he turned into our driveway. And did I really
want to look at it? As if I even understand what he is talking about
as the sound of the ambulance siren from the day before
still blares in my head. I ask if pictures are allowed with
my cellphone. "Unacceptable," is his response,
as he directs me to empty my pockets
upon a sterile counter before
viewing.

After all the years of Billy's
lies, yelling and hitting
I figure his heart will
have sharp edges
pointed corners
and ridges,

but it isn't even bruised.

Leaves

Autumn's first frost
exposes summer's lie.

Winds skim through trees
as black angled swallows
swoop in loops of disbelief.

Ancient oaks and maples cry
in shocking orange, red
and yellow dye.

Knowing their demise I grieve
the deadly price paid by leaves.

Sighting An Owl

the owl sat high sat high
above my little woods
and there we met eyes
instinctively I stood

her gaze seemed sad I'm sure
seeking more than man
a natural connoisseur
starving for lack of land

she glides on wings on wings
retreating feathers wide
and me aching for things
man cannot define

What Remains

The rain fell anyway
on red roses
she'd snipped
on her way
to say goodbye

The rain fell anyway
as she morns alone
in their empty home
he in a hospital room
with fluorescent moons

The rain fell anyway
her head cradled in hands
that soon held the man
as his eyelashes fluttered
one last time

The rain fell anyway
as he forgot everything
they ever knew
leaving her everything
that would never be

Dangerous Haiku

Walking along the
cracked sidewalk I stumble lose
my balance decide

the neighborhood is
not the best. I shouldn't have
acted so careless

except a famous
Haiku poet lives near this
scary bad perilous street.

Wanting to observe
him to feel the excitement,
I stifle every

warning responding
instead to the longing in
my impulsive head.

They assault me with
wood clubs and tire irons.
How mindless, I think.

Blood is gurgling
out my mouth when I spot the
poet down the street.

I sacrificed all
and he watches me die with-
out batting an eye.

If

I just keep walking
dropping to the ocean floor
opening that silent door
weeping wounds would die
by the wet grave
of seaweed's feet

endings are
so final
so deep

Reclusive Lover

a pale blue linen hangs
on his bathroom door
in folds from a vintage hook
French hems hold up the ends
of an elegant dressing gown
masculine and smart it never

touches

the ground and like the man it commands
attention a shroud waiting to cover exposure

nothing

is revealed here until the door is closed
then a hint of scent rises from a satin collar
while royal sleeves slap gently above
the marble floor before falling into place
silent and still once more

Even Now

They found me after a band of Apaches attacked and burned the stagecoach. Time healed my body and mind as I watched his people live a quiet truth. No longer dreaming of home.

A mist rose above the tops of the tents greeting the hunter's moon the night we camped below the ridge. Horses snorted and old men snored while babies cried. His timid touch warmed my heart his hair held the scent of sweet grass and for the first time I slept beneath a warrior's blanket. For the first time I was at peace. But I should have known there is no happy ending.

I cried as my husband's Calvary slaughtered the entire tribe. He thought they were happy tears that I wanted to go home. Women I grew up with, old friends asked what it was like there. How could I tell them that our silent god lived among the savages?

Even now as the white man known as my husband lies sleeping I feel the drum beats of my heart. Remember walking through tall grasses and how the thunder of free buffalo made me ache inside.

Even now, as I raise the barrel of the gun.

Our Father

It wasn't his
station in life I
recall, but his
heavy footsteps.
I was five when
it started. My
bed was in the
lonely corner of
a dreadful
orphanage.
Away from others who pointed and whispered. I discovered that once a week for three
years establishes a pattern of reactions. So I'm well suited for how I earn a living now,
always satisfying every customer by how I react to moves without making a sound.
And they never
question me
when I ask them
to remove their
shoes. But
sometimes I still
cry when kind
ones reach up to
touch my
tarnished
cross.

In the Shadow of Fermilab

Kissing 101

Pavlov's dogs
Pandora's box
and you

electrical storms
roller coasters
lonely nights
the long goodbye

less stress
new beginnings
buy a dog

there is poetry in saliva

Bookstore Relativity

I think I saw the concept
of relativity once while
browsing through a bookstore
not trying to prove anything

an elderly clerk began tap
dancing to the strains of an
old Victorian record
player moving like a
much younger man

in a pinstriped suit
and wingtips he created
physical movements
scattering rays of sun
light that were reaching
through dusty window
panes while he displaced
the reality of our encounter

Formulaic

Sitting in my divorce attorney's office
while browsing a physics book:

Freefall (Equation) $s = \frac{1}{2}gt^2$.

*Where (s) and (t) are the vertical distance and time of fall
and where (g) is the acceleration of gravity:*

Yeah, let's forget the emotion
stick with science.

We are the (s) and your cheating is the (t),
everything else is (g).

your buddies
your drinking
your momma
your this and your that

F
 R
   E
     E
       F
        A
          L
            L

Poetry vs Math

In literature class, I didn't get it.
The metaphors, alliterations
and onomatopoeia.

The dedicated teacher wore
wire rim glasses and dresses
older than me. But her husband
was my sexy math teacher
and algebra formulated itself
into my adolescent heart.

How could she stand there all
prim and proper quoting similes
while he was caught up in formulas
and equations and me
dreaming of irrational numbers?

Today, everything has changed.
I write poetry and math? It makes
me nostalgic and I figure some
in my head but now it's about
statistics and all those lost probabilities.

Splitting Atoms

I'm spinning out
of control again
in an orbit of labor

stellar elements
attempt to mutate
Jungian addictions
as they mimic
a pregnant chaos

and while
as a human form
one cannot recreate
five points of a star

a soul might
deploy memories
of trauma
to breach
its own nucleus
creating the possibility
of a new future

Star Gravity

If you were a beam of light
and I a black neutron star
gravity would make you bend
as you passed my sweet pulsar

Then as your single beam curved
embracing my orb'd terrain
would you risk a stellar eclipse
exploring my dark domain

I Am Not Your Counselor

If you can't be a poet, be the poem.

- *David Carradine*

She Did Not Teach Me Love

She did not teach me love
How could she have known
She knew only coping games
Denials kept her numb

From her I learned to question
Never accept or trust
That dreams were meant for others
They were never intended for us

My life became a sentence
Served with a suffering smile
Until years of self-reflection
Released this wounded child

Today, I wish my mother love
In memories I've set her free
God will forgive Mommy's sins
Her penance was paid by me

Peppermint

"She died in the fetal position,"
his voice was soft.
We were sitting outside an ice cream shop
on a warm September evening.

Taking a bite from his cone
he did not apologize
for his bluntness,
looking straight at me
as if I would challenge her death.

Speaking of our past, our hurts
I wasn't sure how to comfort him
then noticed rain falling
filling our eyes.

Reaching out my hand
I pulled his cone to my mouth
tasting our sweet sadness of life.

City Nurse

Monthly visits with Momma are harder than
shifts on the trauma ward. As an intern, issues
overwhelmed me. But soon I discovered
they were all the same problem;
does a body have air or not?

Shrugging off gritty exhaustion
after a double shift is simply
taking a hot shower, sleeping for hours.

But being with Momma on the farm
is not so easy. Everything, old
and wounded, yet her cotton
dresses still sway on clothes
lines in the yard full
of her air body.

Driving home, it becomes
cockleburs bursting with
memories of the past;
attached like sticky
weeds caught in
the fur of her cats.

Rain

While planting pansies we watch
roofers install a new tiled roof
on a neighbor's home.

"The test will be when it rains," he said
and the rain does come down in sheets
violent for this season.

When he leaves me rain
is still pounding on window panes
there is no slamming doors for us
no shouts no doubts for him.

And the rain keeps falling
as the recent planted pansies
drown in their own flower beds.

Survivor's Psych Nurse

what do I know of your pain
as you sit rigid and alone
and what gain
would there be to name
your fears

I have no energy to peer
behind your survivor's mask

I am not your counselor

and yet somewhere beneath
my mother's breast is a longing
to sneak a peek at that little guy
who cooed
that precious child that was
before they messed with you

Closed Windows

snow melts into spring
as your memory seems
to wander from room to room

silent like when you
were alive but rigid
like flesh approaching death

the hot round sun
cracks into a brooding
storm but all I know is rain

pounding against window
panes you closed
to keep pain
from our home
and now the old
wood moans
as I pry open
every one

Dark Night

the raccoon was there
as I pulled into the drive
dark circled eyes
mirroring mine

it seemed to be waiting
to intervene
with the final plans
of a suffering man

taken by surprise I froze
when it scurried through
dry crackling leaves
frosted with snow

touching the tip
of my shoe
with a furry paw
it then looped away
like a Crow Indian
counting coup

Suds

we had the conversation
three nights before Christmas
sitting on the blue sofa
I bought when my mother died

after he leaves
washing empty cups
I see
my reflection

in a delicate
soap bubble

startled
at the sight

of beauty
without him

Silence

is heavy so I walk along
the river bank bracing
against March winds
startled by the scent of earth
from the woods wondering
if you've noticed spring

I find I'm holding
my breath waiting
until time begins
to breathe with me
and we watch the sun
light rays crawl up the wall

later moonlight is there
a gentle breeze
I fluff our pillows
as silence lays down
next to me

Notes

Dangerous Haiku (page 20): Haiku is a type of poem that uses a meter of 5-7-5

Dead Orchids (page 2): Inspired by my Mother's love of Orchids

Dead Orchids (Cover, title page & page 48): A painting by Catie Barron

Fermilab Photo (page 27): credit to Haley Stein while attending a lecture titled "Dark Matter"

Formulaic (page 30): Freefall equation verified by Fermilab in Batavia, Illinois

If (page 21): Photo credit to Leilani Haag taken on the island of Oahu, Hawaii

Leaves (page 17): Photo credit to the author taken at Nelson Lake, Illinois

Loud Painting (page 3): Inspired while touring Starved Rock, Illinois

Out Of Print (page 6): When an out of print book is for sale the cover is removed

Popcorn (page 10): Inspired after a reading by Billy Collins from Picnic Lightning, in Joliet, Illinois

Sighting An Owl (page 18): Published in Red Owl Magazine, inspired by author Loren Eiseley

Outside the box (page 14): http://www.searchquotes.com/search/

Suds (page 45): The physics of soap bubbles was discussed with a scientist at Fermilab in Batavia, IL

About the Author (page 49): Photo credit to Haley Stein

Dead Orchids is based on a poem by Kitty Jarman, for the 2013 *Art In Your Eye* festival's **Drawn With Words**, held in Batavia, Illinois. This piece is inspired by Kitty Jarman's poem.

For more about Catie Barron's artwork visit www.catarzina.com.

This is Kitty's first published collection of poems. Although many are very personal, she is a writer of fiction. However, she wrote about her mother's love of Phalaenopsis, the moth orchid in the poem "Dead Orchids." That poem was submitted to the 2013 Art In Your Eye festival, held in Batavia, Illinois. It was chosen by artist Catie Barron of catarzina.com, who painted the poem to life. Kitty contacted the artist by phone offering to purchase the painting. After a few weeks with no contact, Kitty called her again and she asked for more time with the excuse that she was extremely busy. "Can we put it off for a week or so?" At this point, Kitty was concerned. Perhaps the artist had a wealthier buyer. Several days later, Kitty came home from work and the painting was hanging on her living-room wall. Her twin daughters, Jennie and Julie, purchased the painting as a marvelous gift. It still hangs in her home. There is life in art and there is art in living.

About the Author

Kitty Jarman grew up near the sea on Oahu, Hawaii. Now settled near the prairies of Northern Illinois, writing contributes to her curiosity about life. Involved with the Fox Valley writing community for many years, she is currently working on a short story collection and a mystery novel. You can contact the author at: shypoet51@yahoo.com.

www.ingramcontent.com/pod-product-compliance
Lightning Source LLC
Chambersburg PA
CBHW070458050426
42449CB00012B/3029